I0211783

BLOOD MOON

Carol Dine

Edited by Jennifer Barber,
Linda Cutting, Tehila Lieberman

Červená Barva Press
Somerville, Massachusetts

Copyright © 2025 by the estate of Carol Dine.

All rights reserved. Poems in this book can be reprinted only by permission of the co-editors, Jennifer Barber, Linda Cutting, and Tehila Lieberman, and may not be reproduced for publication in book, magazine, or electronic media of any kind, except in quotations for the purpose of literary reviews or articles.

Červená Barva Press
P.O. Box 440357
W. Somerville, MA 02144

editor@cervenabarvapress.com
http://www.cervenabarvapress.com

Visit the bookstore at:
http://www.thelostbookshelf.com

Production: Allison O'Keefe
Cover Image: SoHyun Bae, *Jasper Lake: Wings*, 2011, rice paper and pure pigment on canvas, 200 x 150 cm

ISBN: 978-1-950063-96-3
LCCN: 2024946889

CONTENTS

The editors of *Blood Moon* wish to dedicate this volume to the Glazer family, Douglas, Janet & Stella.

BLOOD MOON

Introduction

The three of us—Jennifer Barber, Linda Cutting, Tehila Lieberman—first met Carol Dine, and one another, at The Writers' Room of Boston, a quiet workspace downtown. We became close friends and, through the years that followed, shared our works-in-progress. As a result, we were aware that Carol had completed a nearly final draft of a new poetry collection in the fall of 2019, before a recurrence of her cancer began to take a greater toll on her.

By March of 2020, she had been transferred from a Boston hospital to a hospice house in Needham. During our visits to her, we asked if she would like us to look over her manuscript, entitled *Blood Moon*, and prepare it to be considered for publication, and she quickly agreed, signing a letter of permission.

Over the next three years, as co-editors, we convened monthly via Zoom to go over Carol's manuscript poem by poem, line by line, resolving any issues we had, always keeping Carol's aesthetic of lyric intensity and narrative thrust in mind.

Part 1 of *Blood Moon* highlights the lives of women who acted courageously under the most extreme of circumstances—in the face of repressive regimes, war, disappearances, and exile, often risking their lives to save others and to provide new hope. Part 2 focuses on women artists whose work reckons with the onset of war, personal betrayal at the hands of loved ones, and the twists and turns of recent history.

Everywhere in Carol's poetry, one feels the necessity of art, its ability to probe and transform experience. We are honored that Carol trusted us with finalizing *Blood Moon*, and we are delighted that Carol's dear friend, artist SoHyun Bae, provided the cover image—a piece that Carol loved—for this volume. We want to express our gratitude to Gloria Mindock for her belief in this book, and for guiding it into print. Carol Dine died on March 17, 2020. We miss her. We treasure the time we have spent and continue to spend in the company of her poems.

PART 1

TESTIMONIES

Oh my friends,
In times like these,
Self-control has no meaning.
Rules of reverence do not apply.
Evil is a pressure that shapes us to itself.

> — Sophocles, 5th century BC
> Electra

missiles from the sky...
There is a total lunar eclipse tonight...
the eclipse turns red.
A blood moon.

> — Samar Yazbek, *A Woman in the Crossfire:*
> *Diaries of the Syrian Revolution,* 2012

My Mother's War

—Tania, on her mother, Violette Szabo, France

In the keepsake box, lined with velvet,
a photo, in fading black and white:
I'm wearing my mother's
Croix de Guerre with Silver Cross
pinned to my cotton schoolgirl dress.

In another photograph,
a bronze plaque marks the alley at Ravensbruck,
winter, 1945, where she was executed.
Violette Szabo, code name, Louise.

I imagine her parachute,
a wild white mushroom opening over fields
in Occupied France, the sussac grasses
furrowed by footprints. The German soldier
who wounds her offers a cigarette;
she spits in his face.

In the camp,
she's clad in a thin blue dress
and ankle chains. The commandant
whips her again and again.
"Tell me their plan."
She offers only a poem in code
left on a fragment of silk:

The life that I have
Is all that I have
And the life that I have
Is yours.

Mother Maria

—Mother Maria Skobtsova, Russia, France

Hail Maria,
blessed art thou
among the Jews,
blessed is the borrowed
yellow star on your arm,
the stolen fruits
in the folds of your skirt.

Hail Maria,
blessed your vacant womb,
blessed art thou among
the women on the train.

Hail Maria,
the Lord is with you
in the line of women
waiting in Ravensbruck.
Blessed are your prayers
eclipsing the chimneys.

Doaa

—Doaa al Zamel, Syria, Crete

As if dreaming,
we stepped onto a trawler on the Nile,
two teens escaped from Syria
among five hundred Sudanese, Palestinians, Libyans
who'd traded everything they had
for passage to Europe.

Days later in the deep,
darkness circled us;
an unnamed ship rammed our stern.

I heard moaning, splashing.
Listening for the voice of my beloved,
I cried out his name.

Then I was thrashing
in black water,
trying to remember his face.

In the dark, drifting by, flashes of orange.
I pulled a vest toward me.
Near me, a man stopped treading.
Had it been two nights?

At dawn, nothing but ocean.
A grandfather, shivering,
kissed his granddaughter,
passing her to me.
A mother handed me her infant son
like a bundle of foam.

In the rising sun, the dead floated
in their ghost flesh,
their eyes, red glass.

For three days, I twisted in the churning sea,
in the shadows of low clouds,
weightless but for the babies
I carried, tucked into my vest.

They cried, I sang to them:
Sleep, sleep, for your pillow
I give you a pigeon.

Our rescue was somewhere near Crete,
a cargo ship sent by Eleos,
goddess of mercy.

Rifle

—Nahida Rashid, Kurdistan

Two hundred yards to reach the steps.
I crawl through rubble and ash,
behind white sheets that mark the battleground.

Climbing up to the clay-mud roof,
I place the barrel of my rifle
in the peephole gouged from the wall.

Through the scope, I see nothing
but a few barren trees, tumbleweed,
the numb blue sky.

I had kissed my daughter goodbye, her tears like small stones.
Grandmother called out, fa'iinaalshahid in yamut 'abadana,
"The martyr will never die."

Then mortars explode.
Through the smoke, a line of black ghosts
coming at me:

Daesh, crusaders for the caliphate.
I fire, they fall; I watch their blood
mix with sand.

I am here for Rehanna,
left for dead in the desert
after they raped her. And the woman

they beheaded for not renouncing Christ.
I am here for the Yazidi boy
I carried on my back.

He was trapped
at the top of Sinjar Mountain,
starving.

I send this to my own dear daughter:
before they enslave me,
my own sweet bullet will lift me to Allah.

Desaparecida/Disappeared

—Susana Trimarco, Argentina

In the brothel,
I ask the girls:
Have you seen
two men, a gun,
a red car with tinted windows,
my Marita?

They line up
against the wall;
their black nylons
have crooked seams.

I hold up the photograph.
My daughter, grinning,
models her new plaid mini skirt,
her high, shiny boots.

Can the dead walk?
Can the disappeared
touch my skin
for an instant,
like an eyelash
come loose?

Return

—Elisabeth Tomalin, Germany

Often the hands will solve a mystery that the intellect has struggled with in vain. —C.G. JUNG

1937
In Dresden,
I escape
just before the SS
come to the door.

1938
I find work in London
sketching dress patterns:
roses, lilies formed
by circles and triangles
laid over a grid.

1974
At sixty, my own angst
and memories of meeting Jung
lead me to New York
to study psychotherapy.
I draw my dreams in sand:
a patch of sky,
a snake uncoiling.
Sandspiel, Sandplay.

1978
A letter arrives from Germany:
"Bring your work here, to Bonn."
Could I return to the country
that murdered my aunts,
my uncles, my friends?

Could I refuse to treat
the children of Nazis?

Later, at the clinic in Bonn,
a large box of sand on the table,
my patient and I do not speak.
Facing me, she reaches into the sand,
draws a man with numbers on his skinny arm.
From the figure of the Jew
and from her own eyes,
tears like rain.

Medic

—Sgt. Julia Bringloe, U.S.

June, 2011
Kunar Province, Afghanistan

Strapped to the chopper's cable,
I'm spinning in the wind, a wingless bird.
On the rocky soil, I crawl
to the Afghan soldier,
ply him with oxygen, latch him to the hoist.
The cable swings into a tall, spiked pine.
I shield him with my body,
fracturing my leg.
Above us, the co-pilot leans out
from the chopper, reels the soldier in.

A volley of gunfire: insurgents,
below on the ridge;
I dangle on the cable like a rag doll.
Our soldiers on the ground fire back.
Amidst the shower of bullets,
I'm pulled aboard.

In the blue light of the cabin,
ignoring my pain, I take the soldier's vitals,
insert a breathing tube,
run an IV into his arm.
Across from us on a seat, an empty body bag:
not for him, not yet for me.

Comfort Woman

—Kim Bok-dong, South Korea

1940

In Yangsan, I'm fourteen
when Japanese soldiers drag me from my house.
My five sisters look the other way.

In the first tent, I close my eyes.
Forty, fifty men on the cot, on the floor.
Outside, against the barbed wire,
their stink, their rancid stream.

1945

After the war, I leave Singapore for home.
Barren. I drink and chain-smoke.
If I'd been a cat,
I could have licked myself clean.

1992

Almost fifty years later,
when I look in the mirror,
I still see the shame
refracted in the glass.

2013

Still, no apology.
I set up a fund,
hand all my money to the banker.
Reparations, I say, imagining the women
lining up, one by one.
This is for them.

2016

Eighty-nine, in my wheelchair
I'm outside the Japanese embassy in Seoul,
beside a bronze statue of a girl: our symbol.
Barefoot, she wears a *hanbok*,
a yellow butterfly affixed to her breast.
Behind me, the protesters raise their fists,
yelling, "Apology! Reparations!"
The statue cannot feel
the burning we felt between our legs.

2019

At my funeral in Seoul,
mourners crowd the streets.
Holding hundreds of yellow butterflies,
they open their paper wings.

On the Russian Front

—Florence Farmborough, nurse and photographer, U.K.

1910, Moscow

To remember them,
I took a photograph
of the surgeon's daughters
I'd been tutoring.
They stared at my camera,
asked if I'd use it where I was going.

1916, Chertoviche

Outside the dressing station,
the air exploded.
Another soldier was carried in.
Abdominal wound.
I leaned over his stretcher,
injected morphia.
Nothing else to be done.
I held his hand as he died.

In another village,
my long skirt smeared with mud,
I aimed my camera. In the shed,
I developed and printed the plate:

Six soldiers stand in a line;
gas masks cover their faces,
their eyes, black holes;
suspended from the masks,
canisters like giant beaks.

On the roof of the shed,
two kneeling soldiers
overexposed, a blur of ghosts.

1917, Odessa

"Keep together," I whispered to the women
trudging the winter road,
the snow, blackened slush.
Under the Red Guard,
the Red Cross retreated.

Before I sold my camera for rubles,
I took one last photo:

In a house, the new battlefield,
a Bolshevik soldier
rips apart the bedding of the bourgeoisie.
An antique chair lies in pieces
to be used for kindling.

At the railway station,
they inspected my papers.
Later, discarding my uniform
for street clothing,
I was shocked at how thin I'd become.

In Moscow, Red Guards
patrolled the streets.
Rifle-shots, roundups, churches ravaged,
children carted away. The starving
clamored for bread crusts.

"Anglichanka," they called me,
Englishwoman.
I am going home.

*

I will miss Russia. She taught me
the meaning of suffering.

Mirror

—Christine Granville, Poland, U.K.

In my twenties, I curtsied to the audience
as Krystyna Skarbek,
Polish beauty queen, garlanded in roses.

I was thirty-one when Poland fell.
I left my husband, a wealthy diplomat,
to join the Resistance.
As Madame Pauline, I parachuted into southern France.

Agent for the British, code name *Willing*,
I skied the frozen mountains, past German
border patrols, a message tucked into my vest,
a knife strapped to my thigh.

Disguised as my lover's upper-class wife, Madame Cammaerts,
I bribed a guard, walked into the Vichy prison.
"Release him," I said,
"or British reprisals will be swift."

Back when I was his lieutenant,
we had made love in a burning hotel.
Months after he was freed,
he returned to his wife.

*

After Armistice, penniless, stateless,
I was paid to stretch a smile
as a hostess on a cruise liner.
Later, in my room in a north London hotel,
I looked at the war medals in my drawer:
the George Cross, the Croix de Guerre.

In the mirror I faced the ghost of a woman
who could not have been me; soon to be stabbed
through the heart by a man she refused to bed.

*

I was buried at forty-four as Christine Granville
in St. Mary's, London. The Polish Ambassador,
majors and ladies gathered midday at my gravesite.
Little known spy, my final bow.

Enigma

i. Sheila MacKenzie Lawn, U.K.

The night I arrive at Bletchley Park,
I see antennae hiding
in frozen branches of the Wellingtonia tree;
ice crystals cling to the portico.
Shivering in my thin coat,
I step into oversized footprints in the snow.
In the doorway, a silhouette.

I follow the trainer's shadow through Gothic rooms, past
makeshift offices, all the windows
covered with tape. I trail his lantern
up the winding staircase,
climb over ropes of wire
into the narrow water tower: Station X.

Later, at the keyboard, I type the letter 'A';
the input lamp lights up 'E'.
My message goes into the scrambler, comes out
in German. The air releases its breath.
What I uncover at nineteen
I will never tell my mother,
or the engineer working in a nearby hut,
who will one day be my husband.

ii. Diana Plowman, U.K.

He guides me through the meadow behind the mansion.
Everywhere,
single story brick and wooden huts,
chimneys spewing inky smoke.
At the station, my boss hands me a document:
the Official Secrets Act.
"If you enter this work," he says, "leaving is forbidden."

Hut 4, midnight shift, clicking away. A transmission comes in:
'Nichts neues zuberichten,' 'Nothing new to report.'
Then, in the silence, like ice cracking,
a message from the Commandant: 'Wo ist die Bismark?'
A pause. The response: 'Vor der kuste von Gronland.'

Stunned, my fingers find the keys,
relaying its position to our warships: 'Off the coast of Greenland.'
48 hours later, we spill from our huts, cheering the news:
"The Bismark has been located."
I imagine billows of white smoke smothering the stern,
the mammoth ship keeling, engulfed in flames.

Equations

—Dorothy Vaughan, U.S.

1943
Camp Pickett, VA, laundry room

In the steam heat, I iron
the olive green shirts, khaki ties
at 40 cents per hour.
University scholar,
teacher of mathematics,
the numbers don't add up.

I worry for my four children
in the city playground,
torn sneakers, old clothes;
for my husband
standing at a bellman's desk
behind the hotel's marble pillars.

In the Greyhound station's
colored waiting room,
I unfold the letter
from the aeronautics lab.

How will it feel working
with white people?

1944
Langley Memorial Aeronautics Lab

At 2 AM, from the plate glass window
outside the cavernous wind tunnel,
I calculate the Reynolds number:
the drag of wind flow over airplane wings.

1946
Hampton Institute, college theatre

Finally made a supervisor of the other women
they called "the colored computers,"
I celebrate with my children
in their Sunday best.
Marian Anderson's voice
rises: "He's got everybody here
in His hands."

1960-1961
Building 1268

Alone in the basement,
dwarfed by the massive IBM,
I feed it equations I've translated
into FORTRAN, the language I taught myself.

Rocket test range, Wallop Island

Over and over, I run the numbers
on the spin of the Scout. No one believed
I could figure it out. Hallelujah—
the rocket tests stable.

Hampton Roads, VA

It's evening. On the porch
of my own wooden house,
from somewhere deep within,
I remember the end of my minister's
sermon: "Verily, I say unto you,
Hereafter ye shall see heaven open."
I smile, looking up into space,
the full November moon.

Her Camera

—Dickey Chapelle, U.S.

1945

In an Australian bush hat, oversized eyeglasses,
tailor-made fatigues, tiny pearl earrings,
I focus my battered Leica.
Sniper bullets like screeching birds
rip past my ears.

Later, lifting the image from the stop bath,
I see my own darkening shadow.

Photograph: *Iwo Jima Under Fire*

War shreds the beach:
sand turns to volcanic ash.
A marine dismantles a striped tent;
his ribs show through his naked back.
On an abandoned tank,
rifles tilt like trumpets.

Photograph: *Hungarian Refugee Flees into Austria*

The woman straddles a log.
Behind her, remains of the Andau bridge.
Above her, the clothesline she's clutching;
Soviet tracer flares illumine the forest.
Eyes half closed, dark overcoat unbuttoned,
she pulls herself across the frozen canal.
Ahead of her on the rope, a tattered knot
quivers like edelweiss.

Photograph: *Helicopter War in South Vietnam*

The chopper brushes the stubbled grass; the rotor still spins.
Above it, a low cloud like a deflated balloon.
The soldiers, small as toys, spill from the fog.

Insignias on their uniforms blur—you can't tell
which side they're on.

***

1965

During Operation Black Ferret
in Quang Ngai Province,
I advance with the platoon.
Just over the hill,
the lieutenant right next to me
trips a booby trap wire.

1966

On the anniversary of my death,
at the foot of the hill in Quang Ngai,
Marines salute my memorial plaque:
"We will miss Dickey. She was one of us."

The Golden Gown

—Yehudit Arnon, Czechoslovakia, Israel

Birkenau

The new arrival who lay pushed up against me on the stone slab cries out in Hungarian in her sleep. I press my hand over her lips. Morning. Facing me, women in pajamas like striped birches. Before the guard arrives, I show them how to stretch, unknotting their bodies.

They come for me in the barracks, take me to a large room. Christmas Eve, candles fluttering, the smell of beer and pine. Soldiers clap their big hands, shouting, "Dance for us." I stiffen. "Nein." A soldier drags me outside to the yard. I grip the icy fence. A curtain of snow falls, covering my bare feet.

In the distance, the rumble of tanks. The Red Army comes closer. German soldiers scatter. It's now or never. *Run.*

*

I'm in the forest, in a dead soldier's coat and boots. Hunched low in the moonless dark, inching from tree to tree, I look up at a single star, afraid to ask God for anything more.

*

On the deck of the ship to Palestine, I gather the orphaned children. We pretend to leap the rolling waves.

*

Karmiel, Israel

My dancers watch me from the wings. Center stage, after the last pirouette, I bend my knees, extend the skirt of my shimmering gown until it is wide as a desert across the floor. The music swells. I lie down, see golden flecks of light on sand. On my bare skin, sun.

Interview with the Kommandant

—Gitta Sereny, Austria, U.K.

April, 1971. Dusseldorf Remand Prison, second floor

Franz Stangl and I sit across from each other in a small windowless room. His breath mixes with smoke from my cigarette. His deep-set eyes narrow; a frown creases his brow. He's wearing a starched white shirt open at the collar, his V-neck sweater, grey, like his thinning hair. His hands are broad, reddish, workingman's hands. Now his fists move across the table toward me; my insides shiver, though I know a guard is just outside the door. I recall the warning of an old friend, a bishop: 'If you expose yourself to the devil, he can invade you.'

I open my notebook. One more day here to try to get some answers—what was it that drove him? Did he ever feel remorse? How does a man become a man who can do what he has done? It was just four months ago that I had seen him in the courtroom. He was seated back from the microphone in the dock, a wooden cube like a pen; a soldier stood guard beside him. He stared into an imaginary wall beyond the courtroom, beyond his wife who'd traveled to hear the verdict. It came down: Kommandant of Treblinka, guilty of murdering 900,000 people, sentenced to life in prison. He would appeal the sentence. I had approached Frau Stangl to ask if I might talk with her husband. I held up my press pass. She hesitated, then nodded her head, saying it might help if people heard his side of the story. She'd ask him.

Now sixty-three, perhaps he was ready to open up. I sensed his intelligence, also his arrogance. Though it was twenty-five years ago, I could still hear the voices of the accused at Nuremberg like distant gongs, their answers by rote: 'just following orders.' Could I get Stangl to tell me why?

***

I ask Stangl my first question. "In spring, 1942, did you know what awaited you in Poland?"

"I knew nothing. I was told that I'd be in charge of constructing Sobibor, to be used solely as a supply camp for the army. They said I was qualified since I'd administered the Euthanasia Programme."

"The programme during which you authorized the death of children?" I ask.

"They were grievously ill; it was merciful," he says.

"At the camp, when the exterminations started happening, how did you feel?"

Stangl clears his throat. "I was working in my quarters in the barracks, away from the forest. I could live without seeing anybody dying or dead."

"What about your wife? Did she ever ask about your work?"

"During my leave, she and our young daughters took a room in the village, near the camp. She told me she'd heard rumors. 'My God,' she said, 'what are you doing?' 'Whatever is wrong,' I said, 'I have nothing to do with it.' There was no other way—I had to lie to her.

"After your leave in Sobibor, what happened next?"

"I met with the SS lieutenant. 'I have a job for you,' he said, 'strictly a police assignment.' I knew right away there was something wrong with it, but I didn't know what. 'You're going to Treblinka,' he said.'"

"Here was your chance. You knew all about Treblinka. Why didn't you tell him you couldn't go on with this work?"

"Don't you see? I had no idea if my family was safe. He could have been holding them as hostages."

"What were the lieutenant's exact orders?"

"The lieutenant told me, 'We've already sent 100,000 Jews to Treblinka, and nothing has arrived here in money or materials. Find out where it's disappearing.'"

I ask Stangl about the day he arrived at Treblinka. He begins to sweat, lowering his head. After a pause, he says, "We began to see bodies, hundreds of them, lying there in the heat."

At 5:30 p.m., the guard leads me outside. Feeling feverish, I wait at the Dusseldorf station for the train to Cologne, where I'm staying with friends. The platform is empty and dark. A train approaches, slowing down on the track. I hear children crying and I see small pale faces pressed against the openings in the cars. I pass out. A railway worker helps me up. "It was a freight train," he tells me. "It was carrying calves."

That night I sit down to dinner with my friends. When I speak, it's as if my voice is not my own. After the meal is done, Ruth-Alice tells Klaus and the children to go to the study. "What's wrong?" she says, when we're alone. "You haven't eaten a thing."

I tell her about the freight train. "Honestly, I don't think I can go on."

Ruth-Alice takes my hand. "You know, our children asked what you're doing here; we explained. Gitta, your work is so important. The children told their teachers about it; now they're having discussions at school."

***

The next morning, I return to continue the interview with Stangl.

I notice right away that he has not shaved. Maybe I'm getting to him. I walk toward the table, aware that I'm standing straighter than usual.

"There were 200 children from the Warsaw Jewish Orphanage in Treblinka. What did you feel when you saw them?"

"I just don't remember a group of children like that," Stangl says.

"I ask you, would it not have been possible in Treblinka to express that you were conflicted?"

"I talked to another officer about it. If I had made public what I felt, and had been killed, it would have made no difference. It would all have gone on just the same, as if it and I had never happened." He is looking down at his trembling hands.

"Do you honestly believe that you bear no responsibility?"

"My conscience is clear...about what I did," he says. "I've never intentionally hurt anyone."

"What is God to you?"

"God is faith. I don't understand, but I believe."

"Was God with you in Treblinka?"

Stangl does not answer. He clears his throat. My time for these talks is running out, and my patience is fraying. I hear the guard pacing by the door.

"How do you face yourself?" I ask.

I watch as he grips the table. I ask no more questions.

Then, almost in a whisper, he speaks. "I was there, so yes, in reality, I share the guilt."

He pauses. In his silence, I feel my heart beating. I had what I'd come for.

He looks around the small room, then stares at me. "These talks...it is enough now. Let this be over."

***

Days later, the prison governor leads me into Stangl's cell. He'd died of heart failure nineteen hours after our final conversation. Before his appeal was heard. Beside his cot, a book from the prison library he'd marked with pieces of paper. Its title, *Laws and Honour*.

PART 2

ARTISTS, OPENING

...in solidarity with each thorn...
our bodies opening and closing eager,
breathing the dark impossible.

> —Safiya Sinclair, *Dreaming in Foreign*,
> 2016

Painted Windows

—after Charlotte Salomon, Germany

Once, before my bedtime story,
my mother told me she wanted
to be a winged angel. I remember her
wearing a gossamer white nightgown day and night.

*

In gouache, I paint
the bedroom window she leapt from;
the sky in pre-war Berlin
a cloudless, mottled blue.

*

In wartime, when Grandmother
heard the soldiers knocking on doors
in Villefranche, she flung herself
from a window toward the waves.

*

I mix yellow, citrine green
for the billowing curtains,
blacken Grandmother's silhouette
lifting over the sill.

*

September leaves are falling,
the arrests coming closer.
What color is death?
I pick up my brush to azure the sky.

Her Armor

—Rose Valland, France

In the basement of the Jeu de Paume,
I watch Goering as he lifts Bruegel's *Hay Harvest*
to an easel; under a blue horizon, peasants in miniature
walk over wheat turning to gold.

Stopping in front of a wooden rack,
he grins at Leger's *Woman in Red and Green*;
her head, a helmet,
her body armor striped red.

He fails to see my camera
quickly recording the theft: Cezanne, Gaugin,
Lautrec, Matisse, Renoir. The names of the owners—
Kann, Rosenberg, Rothschild, Schloss—
folded in my pocket.

Later in my room, I signal my contact, "Halt the train."
The frames shift in their nailed crates.

The Wounded Table/*La Mesa Herida*

—after Frida Kahlo, Mexico

Have you seen my painting?

2 x 8 meters, it disappeared
through the walls in Warsaw.

You cannot mistake me
rooted as I am at the center;
a smiling skeleton twirls
a strand of my long dark hair.

Behind me, my Judas
in papier-mâché,
dressed in blue overalls:
...behold the hand of him that betrayeth me

Facing each other, the witnesses—
Granizo, my pet fawn,
Antonio and Isolda, nephew and niece,
children of my empty womb.

The table's feet are bandaged;
blood-paint seeps from their wounds.

Large, bone-white fingers
press down hard on the wooden table
to keep it from rising.

Lost and Found, 1946-1964

—Ardelia Ripley Hall, Cultural Officer, Washington, D.C.

Photographs of art
scattered across my desk. My work
is to scour Europe for the missing.

No. 340 *Van Gogh, The Harvest*
The rolling wheat fields, parted like a river.

Returned to Folkwangmuseum, Essen.

No. 886 *Da Vinci, Lady with an Ermine*
The ermine, I recall, a symbol of purity.

Returned to Czartoryski Museum, Krakow.

*

In last night's dream,
I stood beside the American soldiers
deep in the Merkers salt mine,
watching them hoist the canvas
to a ledge. Lit by a single lantern,
Manet's *Wintergarden*:
in a pleated blue dress,
a woman on a bench
gazes beyond her husband,
past the lush greenery.

*

No. 242 *Matisse, Woman Seated in Armchair*
I study another image.
The woman wears a floral blouse,
a gossamer hood covering her head.
It looks like she's floating backward
into the patterned wallpaper.

Whereabouts unknown.

She

—after Alison Saar, U.S.

A Black woman, carved
from graphite and wood
hangs upside down from a rope, feet bound.

Elbows by her side,
hands crossed
above her rounded breasts.

Her head
has sprouted antlers,
splayed against the floor.

The eyes deep, unfinished,
as if the chiseled
agony still goes on.

Necklace

—after Mona Hatoum, Palestine, U.K.

A wooden torso
on a podium.
Around it, a necklace
made of human hair.

You can still see the fissures
in the bleached red oak.

My art, always in the wrong
place. In exile,
I cut my auburn hair.

With the point of the shears,
I pricked an index finger,
pulled the strands

through droplets of blood.
Winding each strand in a circle,
I sewed them together, thick as nests.

In the spaces where light
struggles to breathe,
I hear the children's voices:

Let me run outside
toward the olive trees,
follow my shadow
until I am home.

Cells

—after Mona Hatoum, Palestine, U.K.

Sixteen steel cages
stand in a block on the bare floor,

each with its own lock.
Inside, organisms

of red glass.
Wombs? Human hearts?

The light goes both ways:
from the steel onto the glass,

from the glass onto the steel,
as if the artist

were standing guard
over what she has imprisoned.

Siluetas/Silhouettes

—after Ana Mendieta, Cuba, U.S.

i.
I'll return in blood-paint.
Santa Muerte, goddess of death,
my body imprinted
on a sheet
in a fissured portal,
candlewood branches
arcing at my feet.

ii.
My art, my sex
enraged him.
He shoved me
through the window's glass;
I spilled across Manhattan.

iii.
Beside the ocean
my open hands, vermilion,
imprint the sand.
The tide comes,
washes the rest of my body
clean.

The Travelers

—after Marie-Lousie von Motesiczky, Austria, U.K.

I paint us fleeing Vienna in a wooden boat shaped like my father's stringless cello. My mother stares into breaking waves, her hair turned to foam. Black tears stain the face of my brother's ghost from Auschwitz. In the center, naked, I'm holding the rolled canvas I grabbed from the studio. A bronze mirror, adorned with pearl rosettes, is propped up against the stern. Dressed in a silken gown, our neighbor leans into her own reflection gone mad.

Vigil

—after Irina Korina, Russia

I hear their boots
crunch in the frozen marsh
as prey senses a herd of wild boar.

When I return home,
my window's open;
severed wires
snake over my bedside table.

There must be a hidden camera;
it clicks, zooms in,
noting the size of my wrists
for the handcuffs they'll use.

I stay in my room with my brushes,
vodka, salt cheese, black bread.

In semi-darkness,
I paint my face
again and again
on the wallpaper
to blend with the pattern
of green birds and leaves.

From the wall,
all of my eyes
keep watch.

Two Paintings

—after Nancy Spero, U.S.

Gunship

I mark the horizon line.
The helicopter hovers
over a village;
from the American eye of
the pilot,
from the apocryphal belly of the beast,
napalm spills
over a mother father child. Their
arms and spoons scatter. Their
paper skin burns.

Male Bomb

With light brown gouache,
I diffuse
half the male torso
in smoke.
Below, between his open legs,
the serpentine cock erect,
carnage spewing
from its mouth.
I work
sheet after opaque sheet
until the paint
runs out.

Carrying the Enemy

—Tamara Stepanovna Umnyagina, Russia

Two wounded men in the smoke near Stalingrad—
I'd carry one for a bit, set him down, go back for the other.
They had both been hit high up on the legs and were losing blood.
Minutes were precious, every minute.

When I crawled away from the battle and there was less smoke,
I realized I was carrying one of our tank men and a German...
That accursed uniform. Our people are dying there,
and I'm saving a German! They were scorched black, identical.

I lifted our wounded man and thought: 'Should I go back
for the German or not?' I knew that if I left him, he would die.
I crawled back for him.
                    I went on carrying both.

My Body is My Art

a play in three acts

—Marina Abramović, Bulgaria, U.S.

Prologue:
In Bulgaria, my parents, Communist soldiers,
hit me so I'd obey. My playmates
were shadows; I talked to invisible things. I came from faraway stars,
a shaman told me, to teach humans how to not feel pain.

Act I:
I scream until I lose my voice.
Kneeling, I whip my naked back with leather straps.
I lie down in the middle of a wooden five-pointed star, the star on fire.

Act II:
You're seated in rows on the floor in the dark.
Close by, a ladder tilts toward a platform
on the stage where I stand naked,
my hands wide open by my sides. Inches above me,
a metal shower head drenches me.

Act III:
Pain is keeping a secret.
In a roped-off space,
I sit on a wooden chair
at a small square table.
One by one you sit down
across from me
in the empty chair.
For fifteen minutes,
we gaze into each other's
eyes. Sometimes you

cry, or place a hand
over your heart.

Often, you wait in line outside
until morning.

During the third month,
I wear all white, as if holy.
The table is gone,
nothing between us.
I breathe in deeply,
warm air from outside,
inside; no thought,
no feeling,
a full emptiness.

Her Drawings

—after Helga Weiss, Czechoslovakia

December, 1941
Prague

"List of Possessions"

My mother is removing
her mother's silverware
from the open drawer.
Bent over the desk nearby,
my father scrawls numbers.
Plants in the bookcase
turn their leaves
toward the window light.

April, 1943
Terezin

"The Departure of a Transport"

The Ghettowache, ghetto guards
have taken Daddy away.

One guard salutes with a gloved hand,
another shoulders a rifle.
The people behind them have no faces.
The horizontal lines are rain.

November, 1944
Auschwitz

"Counting"

They write everyone down; for safety's sake,
Mother takes off four years. At fourteen, I add three.
We never tell anyone we're mother and daughter.

Two guards stand at the bunks
counting the three rows of naked legs
as if in a burlesque show.
Some cross at the ankles.
Some women hide their bare feet
beneath straw blankets.
Mother's legs and mine,
skinny trunks of white birch.

Epilogue, December, 2012
Prague

Now at eighty-eight, in the flat where I was born,
I remove the yellowing paper from the desk drawer--
the diary and my drawings. My dear uncle,
who'd been assigned to keep
the records in Terezin, hid them
with other documents in the barracks wall;
after the war, he returned to find them,
brought them back to me.

In one drawing, I see Father again, wrapped in his bedroll
in the Prague courtyard, the morning of the roundup.

I stare into another drawing, people rushing toward
the tower at Mauthausen, the fluttering of a small white flag.

I speak aloud to my father:
"Daddy, I have survived."

Where I Live

—Yayoi Kusama, Japan

Tokyo, 1939

At ten, I saw dots everywhere;
like stutters, they filled the flowers I painted,
the field, my father's unfaithful eyes.
"Stop," my mother said.

New York City, 1958

From the airplane, I saw nets
strangling the ocean.

The galleries turned me down:
dots falling from my canvases,
mirrored spheres,
white phallic sculpture.
Warhol and Oldenburg copied me.

I jumped from the apartment window,
didn't know then why I was spared.

New York City, 1969

An antiwar happening,
"Grand Orgy to Awaken the Dead."
I arranged the naked protesters
by a fountain,
dotted their bodies in red.
"Publicity, not art," the critics wrote.

Tokyo, 2018

In the mental hospital,
I dye my hair flame orange.
They stand in lines
all over Europe, I'm told,
and in Matsumoto, where I was born,
for my landscapes
clotted with broken wings,
snakes climbing a red dotted wall.

Floating Lanterns

—after Toshi Maruki, Japan

Days after the bombing,
I caught the first train back.
Everything was flattened:

smoldering wood, plaster, bone;
a few trees, now sticks
bent over the ashen road.

I looked beneath the railroad bridge: where once there was water,
bodies climbed the riverbed.

My own house, a skeleton.
I searched for food, patched my roof
with sheets of scorched tin.

*

For three years, I do not draw or paint.
When it's time, I begin
with my own nude body:

in charcoal dust, I sketch my
breasts, thighs, pubis

on paper I made by hand,
using weeds and strands of my hair.

On the 6th of August,
I meet the others at the riverbank,
each of us holding an orange lantern,

a lit candle inside.
Some are painted with names

of the departed; I place my drawing in one.
We release the lanterns to the water—
their illuminated shadows

float down the seven rivers of Hiroshima
on their way out to the ragged sea.

Reconstruction

—after SoHyun Bae, U.S.

Canyons erupt to
bedrock.

Cumulus clouds
shed their skin.

Traces of missile,
human bone, feather.

The wind takes a last breath,
sputters out

stilled shadows in black ice,
crystalline cave markings.

Stalactites dangle
in bottomless space.

The stars are swallowed,
emptiness in their wake.

        Then the glacial mouth
        opens again,

        pure blue flame
        roaring

        into the darkness,
        the light.

ACKNOWLEDGMENTS

Thanks to the editors of the following journals in which these poems first appeared:

Austin Poets International, di-verse-city Anthology: "Necklace"
Bitter Oleander: "My Body is My Art," "Reconstruction,"
       "Travelers," and "Vigil"
Ekphrasis: "Floating Lanterns"
Forgotten Women: A Tribute in Poetry (anthology), ed. Ginny
       Lowe Connors: "Desaparecida/Disappeared"
Inkwell: "She"
*Liberation: New Works on Freedom from Internationally
       Acclaimed Poets* (anthology), ed. Mark Ludgwig: "Doaa"
Lilith: "Her Armor" (as "Resistance")
Minerva Rising: "My Mother's War"
Norman Mailer Review: "The Golden Gown" and "Interview
       with the Kommandant"
Pangyrus: "Siluetas/Silhouettes"
Salamander: "The Wounded Table/La Mesa Herida"

SOURCES AND FURTHER READING

Part One

Violette Szabô

Tania Szabô, *Young, Brave and Beautiful: The Missions of Special Operations Executive Agent Lieutenant Violette Szabô, George Cross, Croix de Guerre avec Étoile de Bronze* (The History Press, 2015).

Mother Maria Skobtsova

Sergei Hackel, *Pearl of Great Price: The Life of Mother Maria Skobtsova* 1891-1945 (St. Vladimir's Seminary, 1981).

Maria Skobtsova, *Essential Writings*, Modern Spiritual Masters (Orbis Books, 2002).

Doaa al Zamel

Melissa Fleming, *A Hope More Powerful Than the Sea: The Journey of Doaa Al Zamel* (Flatiron Books, 2017).

Nahida Rashid

Marine Olivesi, "Meet the female colonel leading Kurdish forces into battle against Isis" (www.theworld.org), August 7, 2014.

Simon Valentine, "Meet the Kurdish Female Warrior Who Battles Isis" (www.stream.org), May 18, 2016.

Susana Trimarco

Scott C. Johnson, "Argentina's Susana Trimarco: One Mother's Fight Against Human Trafficking" (www.newsweek.com), October 29, 2012.

Elisabeth Tomalin

Rachel Dickson, "Elisabeth Tomalin: Émigré Designer 1912-2012." *In Exile and Gender II: Politics, Education, and the Arts* (Brill, 2017).

Julia Bringloe

Erik Sabistan, *Dustoff 7-3: Saving Lives Under Fire in Afghanistan* (Warrior Publishing Group, 2015).

Kim Bok-dong

Documentary Film: *My Name Is Kim Bok Dong*, directed by Won-Geung Song; written by Geun Ra Kim.

Florence Farmborough

Florence Farmborough, *With the Armies of the Tsar: A Nurse at the Russian Front* (Futura Books, 1977).

Christine Granville

Clare Mulley, *The Spy Who Loved: The Secrets and Lives of Christine Granville, Britain's First Special Agent of World War II* (Pan Books, 2013).

Sheila MacKenzie Lawn and Diana Plowman

Sinclair Henry, *The Secret Life of Bletchley Park: In the Words of the Men and Women Who Worked There* (Aurum Press, 2010).

Dorothy Vaughan

Margot Lee Shetterly, *Hidden Figures: The American Dream and the Untold Story of the Black Women Mathematicians Who Helped Win the Space Race* (William Morrow, 2016).

Dickey Chapelle

John Garofolo, *Dickey Chapelle Under Fire: Photographs by the First American Female War Correspondent Killed in Action.* (Wisconsin Historical Society Press, 2015).

Yehudit Arnon

Laure Gilbert, "Dancers Under Duress: The Forgotten Resistance of Fireflies" in *Dance Today*, September 2019, Issue No. 36.

Judith Brin Ingber, "Dancing Despite the Scourge: Jewish Dancers During the Holocaust," www.jbriningber, 2005.

Gitta Sereny

Gitta Sereny, *Into That Darkness: An Examination of Conscience* (Vintage, 1983).

Gitta Sereny, *The German Trauma: Experiences and Reflections 1938-2000* (Allen Lane The Penguin Press, 2000.)

Part Two

Charlotte Salomon

Toni Bentley, "The Obsessive Art and Great Confession of Charlotte Salomon." In *The New Yorker*, July 15, 2017.

Rose Valland

Corinne Bouchoux, *Rose Valland: Resistance at the Museum* (Laurel Publishing, 2013).

Frida Kahlo

www.fridakahlo.org/the-wounded-table.jsp

Ardelia Hall

https://www.monumentsmenandwomenfnd.org/hall-ardelia-r

Alison Saar

www.nmwa.org/art/artists/alison-saar

www.americanart.si.edu/artist/alison-saar-32320

Mona Hatoum

www.tate.org.uk/art/artists/mona-hatoum-2365/who-is-mona-hatoum

Ana Mendieta

www.moma.org/artists/3924

Irina Korina

Ruth Addison, ed., *Irina Korina. The Tail Wags the Comet—New Work* (Art guide, 2018)

https://irinakorina.com

Nancy Spero

Leon Golub and Robert Storr, *Nancy Spero: The War Series 1966-1970* (Charta, 2004).

Tamara Stepanova Umnyagina

Svetlana Alexievich, *The Unwomanly Face of War* (Penguin Classics, 2017)

https://weeklyworker.co.uk/worker/1196/from-the-mouths-of-the-women/

Marina Abramović

https://medium.com/@lottewayenberg/marina-abramović-my-body-my-project-6dbf1b406b9c

Helga Weiss

https://www.jewishmuseum.cz/en/program-and-education/exhibits/archive-exhibits/88/

https://education.mjhnyc.org/artifacts/artwork-childs-drawing-of-hunger/

Yayoi Kusama

https://www.davidzwirner.com/artists/yayoi-kusama

Toshi Maruki

https://awarewomenartists.com/en/artiste/toshi-maruki/

SoHyun Bae

https://www.navacontemporary.com/artists/40-sohyun-bae/

https://www.sohyunbae.com

ABOUT THE AUTHOR

Carol Dine was a celebrated poet, essayist, and memoirist. Art critic and author John Berger wrote of Dine's *Van Gogh in Poems* (Bitter Oleander Press, 2009), "Her observation of [Van Gogh's] drawings equals his observation of what he was drawing." Dine read from the book at the Van Gogh Museum, Amsterdam, and the Royal Academy of Arts, London. Her memoir, *Places in the Bone* (Rutgers University Press, 2005), which combines prose and poetry, deals with the redemptive power of art. Her poems appeared in numerous literary magazines, including *Aesthetica Creative Arts Annual* (U.K.), *Bitter Oleander*, *Boulevard*, *Inkwell*, *Lilith*, and *Salamander*, as well as within the anthologies *After Shocks: Poetry of Recovery* and *Poems Against War: Bending Toward Justice*.

Dine received a grant from the Barbara Deming Memorial Fund and the Sword of Hope from the American Cancer Society. She lived in Brookline and she taught writing at Suffolk University and the Massachusetts College of Art & Design.

In addition to *Van Gogh in Poems* and *Places in the Bone*, her previous books include *Naming the Sky*, *Trying to Understand the Lunar Eclipse*, and *Orange Night*.

www.ingramcontent.com/pod-product-compliance
Lightning Source LLC
Chambersburg PA
CBHW020215090426
42734CB00008B/1082